5 Ways to Make Money While You Sleep

Other books by this author

PHP5 The Object Factory Model – A strongly typed object oriented design pattern in a weakly typed language. Introducing smart objects in PHP5.

5 Steps to a Successful e-Commerce Site – A guide to successful e-commerce including tips on search engine optimization and social media marketing techniques.

5 Ways to Make Money While You Sleep

Alister Rutledge

Published by Alister Rutledge
2014

Copyright © 2014 by Alister Rutledge

All rights reserved. This book or any portion thereof may not be reproduced or used in any manner whatsoever without the express written permission of the publisher except for the use of brief quotations in a book review or scholarly journal.

First Printing: 2014

ISBN 978-1-291-84393-4

alister.rutledge@bigpond.com.au

Dedication

To Rada
Thank you. Without your loving support this book would not have been written.

Contents

Preface xi

Introduction 15

The Largest Shopping Mall 24

Your Personal TV Station 34

The Best Seller 44

The Killer App 53

Online Trading 61

Conclusion 66

Appendix 1 69

Glossary 82

5 Ways to Make Money While You Sleep

Alister Rutledge

Preface

The current economic climate in Australia was the catalyst that brought this book about. At the time of writing Qantas has just announced it will ax 800 jobs, GM will close its factory with the loss of several hundred jobs, Ford will stop manufacturing cars in Australia and Alcoa aluminum will close operations with the loss of several hundred more jobs. All this in just the state of Victoria. The flow on effects of these job losses will be felt all over Australia for months, maybe years, to come.

The problem of job losses, particularly in manufacturing, is nothing new to the world's developed economies. Jobs have been moving to the world's developing economies for many years. But it's not all doom and gloom. In my opinion the developed economies are moving through a period of transition. I hesitate to put labels on this but, for the sake of clarity, I'll say the transition is from the post-industrial to the digital. This transition has been underway for the last quarter of the 20th century and will likely continue for most of the 1st quarter of the 21st century.

The transition is being driven and simultaneously hindered by large corporations. There are several technologies under development that are going to combine in the near future to speed the transition. These are the 3-D printer, robotics and artificial intelligence. 3-

5 Ways to Make Money While You Sleep

D printing will impact the manufacturing industry to an unknown extent. It will also impact the CAD (Computer Aided Design) professions. It will be possible for individuals to act like entire factories. An individual who creates a CAD package will be able to sell it to anybody with a 3-D printer. I think of it as distributed manufacturing. This is going to change the manufacturing landscape in the developed world but also perhaps stifle the manufacturing industries in the developing world. Although, I think individuals in the developing economies like Africa and Southeast Asia will adopt and adapt to this technology far more readily than those in the developed economies. Developed economies will see this as a threat while developing economies will see this an opportunity. There will also be a lot of work for lawyers specializing in intellectual property and copyright infringement laws.

Take for example the plastic coat hanger. Right now there is a factory producing plastic coat hangers with injection molders. In the near future, if you want a plastic coat hanger, you will be able to download a file and print one off in the same way you print a document today. The example is trivial but the ramifications are enormous. There will be no need for the factory and all the jobs that go with it. There will be no need for the injection molders and all the jobs that go with producing and maintaining that equipment. There will be no need for all the jobs associated with shipping and selling the coat hangers

Advances in robotics are going to continue to impact every sector of society. As robots become more autonomous and more mobile they will continue to impact the manufacturing and services industries. These are two industries that comprise the bulk of jobs in the economies of developed countries. This transition is inevitable but needs to be carefully managed. Combine robotics with AI (artificial intelligence) and you have the potential for exponential growth in robotics and the computer industries in general. AI will change the face of medicine, space exploration, the resources sector. It will be a profound change to society.

At the same time as these advances are being made, large corporations are hindering the pace of change. An example is the hybrid car. A car that runs on a combination of petrol and electricity. A hybrid car is completely unnecessary. Fully electric cars were first developed in the late 19th century. There was a fleet of electric cabs in London in 1897. So electrically powered vehicles are nothing new. Pontiac released a fully electric car in the late 1990s but recalled them when they were found to be so reliable that the auto parts industry was being adversely affected. The only reason we have hybrid vehicles today is the oil industry would be severely

5 Ways to Make Money While You Sleep

affected by a transition to fully electric cars. That would of course affect the world economies as well.

The transition is being felt most by people who have jobs. Employers are not in jeopardy of losing their source of income through no fault of their own. Yet you always hear of the difficulties faced by employers in the news. The real difficulties are being faced by the employees. They are the people whose lives are turned upside down by these redundancies, retrenchments and job losses.

I believe we are living in a unique time. A time when an individual can have the same corporate presence online as the largest corporations. The internet has vast commercial potential and the corporations have been slow to take advantage of it. I used to think that one needed to imitate the corporate model of forming a company and creating a traditional e-commerce business. I have come to realize that this is not necessary. Right now there are several ways to make money while you sleep without investing large amounts of capital. Sleeping and making money at the same time is a life changing experience. To me it means freedom. I want to share what I know about freedom with you. It's my contribution to people successfully handling the transition.

Alister Rutledge

Alister Rutledge

Introduction

This book is intended to be a guide to people who want a better quality of life. I have worked for most of my adult life. I have had several jobs, I even enjoyed some of them. I have come to realize that a job is not the path to wealth. It can be a path to riches but I believe wealth and riches are often mistaken to mean the same thing. Some people become rich by working. Banking executives are a good example of this, as are politicians. For most of us we get paid just enough money to have to keep going back to work at our jobs each day.

It took me a while to figure it out but really our life is actually valued at our hourly rate when we are working at our jobs. When we are not working, our life has no value. I don't like this idea. I see my life as being the most valuable thing I have. People will often tell you your health is the most important thing, but I disagree. My life is the only thing I really have and I am forced to spend one third of it asleep and another third of it working to make someone else wealthy. The other third of my life seemed to be spent either getting ready for work or sleep.

We describe some people as "independently wealthy" but what does this really mean? To me it means they have a source of income that allows them to live comfortably without working. Traditionally an independently wealthy person's income would come from investments. The

5 Ways to Make Money While You Sleep

investments generate money. So what we need is a money generator. Something that will generate enough money to live comfortably on. This book describes 5 ways to create money generators. I personally have made money while sleeping from each one of these methods.

Any research on the web will turn up lots of ways to earn a living from the internet. Some of these will actually be legitimate. Most of the time you will find that you are exchanging one job for another job, often for less money and longer hours. One thing to remember when researching is: the money has to flow from the internet to your bank account. If you find yourself responding to a limited time offer only available to you at a special discount rate then you are likely to be going the wrong way about generating money. There are two important points to be aware of here. Firstly there is the marketing angle. Secondly there is the value adding angle. These two are inter-related.

The marketing angle is very simple, very effective and based on fear and exclusivity. Fear is a very effective way to control people and is a powerful marketing technique. By offering a discount price or exclusive offer for a limited time you are inducing the fear that the customer will lose out on the deal if they don't "act now". This is why you will normally see a "call to action" associated with a limited time offer. These are marketing concepts you need to make yourself familiar with so that you don't succumb to them and you can utilize them in your money generating endeavors.

The value adding angle is where most people looking to make money online trip up. There are very few genuine ways to make money online without starting a business and building a website. There are many people who offer to sell you the software to exploit several popular money making schemes or methods. These people are jumping on the band wagon. They are trying to sell you what is essentially value added products, which is legitimate. What they are promising the products will do is often not legitimate. Most often the promise is that you will gain an edge on the competition if you use their software. This is generally not the case and you are wasting your time and money buying into this false hope.

The number one rule that you must keep in mind at all times is; "the money has to flow from the internet to your bank account." If you cannot see this flow immediately apparent, then listen to the little voice warning you that you are being scammed. This is not to say that you don't have to spend money to make money. In some cases you do. On the web most legitimate ways to make money will cost nothing to setup but may charge a small percentage in fees from the sale.

The internet reflects the real world where making money is concerned. In the real world you sell either a product or

5 Ways to Make Money While You Sleep

a service to make money. It is exactly the same online. Every money making endeavor on the web today is either selling a product or providing a service. Google provides a service with its search engine. FaceBook provides a service with its social network. Amazon sells products. A money generator has to conform to these rules to be successful. The key component to success that all these well-known websites have in common is traffic. Large numbers of people visit these sites on a daily basis.

When I first started surfing the web there were about 5000 websites on the internet. Today there are about 5000 websites published every second. Going live with a website is akin to turning a black light on in a dark room. Nothing happens! In order to get traffic you have to spend money promoting your site. The answer is to go where the traffic goes. This is true in the real world as well. You don't open a restaurant in a rural area. You open a restaurant where people congregate. The same is true for bookstores, electronic shops etc.

Providing a service to people is a difficult thing to set up without spending a lot of time and money. Selling is product is a lot easier to accomplish and there are plenty of services available to help you accomplish this. The question is; what product can you sell? This is a question I can't answer for you. Everyone has a unique set of circumstances that make it impossible for me to provide all the answers regarding exactly what will work for you.

What I can give you a place to start, some ideas that I know will work and places to go to get information so you can do the research that will provide the answers for you specific problems.

Research and planning are two important steps you must take to ensure your success online. Due to the generalized nature of the information presented in this book I have provided space for you to write down the results of your research specific to your situation. In this way you can keep all of the relevant information in one place. I have also provided space for you to outline your plans to achieve your goals. There is also included a glossary that gives you the relevant URLs for the websites I refer you to in the various chapters. Also, I provide a summary of the important points I want you to understand at the end of each chapter so you can keep you research focused.

There are two methods of creating money generators that I am not including in this book but want to mention at this point. They are affiliate advertising and drop shipping. Affiliate advertising is basically making commission on sales. A good resource for this is ClickBank. You sign up for a ClickBank account and get a unique identifier that is recorded when a person clicks on an ad and subsequently makes a purchase. There is a philosophy that says you can collect a few banner ads and email them around the web and make money from sales. The philosophy seems to come from people who are selling the services to do the

5 Ways to Make Money While You Sleep

emailing. From what I have seen, money will flow from your bank account to the internet.

Affiliate advertising is a legitimate way to make money while sleeping but it is not as easy as you think. First there is a lot of competition from other affiliates and also from the company selling the product. You can make very good commissions but you have to have exposure and high volumes of traffic. The traffic needs to be qualified traffic in order to make consistent money. Think of your archetypal vacuum cleaner salesman. I mention affiliate advertising here because, once you find you have time on your hands, you may want to build a website. I see no reason why you should not host a few banner ads on your site.

Drop shipping is definitely a money generator. It describes a wholesaler who will ship a single unit to a customer and more often than not, the wholesaler will package the item with your logo or brand name. Some of the largest online retailers are in fact drop shippers. In other words, the retailer holds no stock! There is simply a website that the customer places an order on and makes payment. The order is emailed to the wholesaler and in some cases the producer, who then ship the product. One resource to look for regarding this is The Drop Ship Source Directory. This is a list of drop shippers and how to contact them. It has been available for more than ten years and costs about $200 to buy.

I have not personally bought the directory and I don't know how accurate it is. I am not including drop shipping in this book as I personally have not tried it. Also, there are a lot of setup overheads associated with drop shipping. First of all drop shippers will only deal with limited liability companies. So you have to register a company before you start. In Australia it will cost about $430 to setup a company. You then need a website that will be able to take payments. The cheapest I can create and host an ecommerce site for is about $1200. The biggest expense being the SSL certificate for secure financial transactions. You then need to get products to sell through the drop shippers. This can be difficult if you don't have a history of selling online. Then there is the issue of driving traffic to the site and getting conversions. It's about return on investment (ROI). You can get a return on your investment with drop shipping but it will probably take a while.

The five ways to make money included in this book require little or no capital investment but they do require an investment in time. If you are working you can invest the time you would normally spend watching TV or chilling out. Spending 10 hours a week trying to make money is a more valuable use of the time you have free. If you are not working, then spend your time making money rather than looking for that job 200 other people want.

5 Ways to Make Money While You Sleep

You also do not need experience to get these five money generators working and you do not need to give up your day job while you start generating money. They are not get rich quick schemes. In only one case you can start making money immediately. They do not require you to build and host a web site. In fact you should avoid building a website as this will add unnecessary complexities and costs. Where there is a small capital investment required I can give you approximate costs for Australia as that is where I have personally spent the time and money required.

One more point I want to make before moving on is that it should be apparent that the internet reflects the real world in that you need to have something to sell in order to make money. There are no magic elixirs or generous millionaires or Nigerian princes who want to give you their money. Money does not grow on trees or fall from the sky. It takes hard work and perseverance to create money generators and more often than not the rewards are to be found in the journey as well as the destination.

Alister Rutledge

5 Ways to Make Money While You Sleep

The Largest Shopping Mall

The first time I made money while sleeping was on eBay. Before you scream and ask yourself "Why did I buy this book?" I want to give you a couple of success stories and explain why these endeavors succeeded. Also, consider that at the time of writing there are approximately 150 eBay millionaires in Australia. There are a lot more people making less than 1 million a year but still living comfortably.

The nephew of a good friend of mine decided to make a video about how to execute several skateboard tricks. He was 14 years old and had not made a video before. It was during the school holidays and his father was not interested in helping him, so he did it all on his own. He burnt a couple of DVDs and put them up for sale on eBay. He made $26,000 in 6 months. His father helped him make a second video about how to execute more advanced skateboard tricks. It included a section on what not to do when the kid broke his leg during filming.

Another friend did even better. This guy was a long-haired hippy lay-about who never did a hard day's work in his life. He did know how to make glass beads that people use in craft work. He decided to sell them on eBay. As you can imagine the market for glass beads seemed pretty small to me and a few others. But no! As it turns out the brewing industry uses glass beads to clean out their pipe work. So it took about 3 years to get the glass bead business making a decent return but my friend persevered and now has a wife and 3 kids and still doesn't do a hard day's work.

So yes it is very possible to make a living off eBay. If you don't like eBay there are other auction sites you can consider. My advice is to start with one site and one product and then expand to multiple auction sites with one product. Then introduce several products across all the sites. Monitor the performance of each product and drop the products that don't perform.

There are a couple of very good reasons that I am suggesting you start with eBay especially if you are new to the web or have not made money online before. In order to implement the number one rule that money must flow from the internet to your bank account you have to put in place the necessary infrastructure to allow this to happen. Ebay does this for you. In order to create an eBay account you require an email address and a PayPal account. I suggest that you create a webmail account like a Gmail, Hotmail or Yahoo account. The reason being is that you probably have an email account provided to you by your ISP. If you change your ISP in the future, which is likely, you will have to update all of your money generators with your new email address. To avoid this hassle you should set up your payment infrastructure the correct way the first time.

5 Ways to Make Money While You Sleep

Setting up a PayPal account takes several days or weeks so you want to get that completed before creating your eBay account. The other reason I am suggesting eBay is about Return on Investment (ROI). You will spend some time setting this infrastructure up. You might as well get a return for this investment. With eBay you are almost assured of getting a sale for almost any product you offer. The reason I say this is that in order to successfully sell a product online you must have that product seen by as many people as possible. Ebay has a very large volume of daily traffic. This means you do not have to consider driving traffic to your products through advertising.

Choose your products carefully. The DVD and glass beads succeeded in part because they are lightweight and durable. This makes them easy to post around the world. It is important to consider the cost of postage when you advertise your products on eBay. You can compete on price if you make profit on postage rates. Offering free postage is actually recommended by eBay. In this case you add the postage rate to the price of the product. Consider adding a postage rate slightly above the average global rate. Ebay has sites in many countries so you are more likely to be posting to national addresses than international addresses. Therefore you will make a profit from postage rates to national addresses and lose less on international addresses.

Choose products that fill a niche. For instance, there is a good market for handmade paper. This is an excellent product to sell online because it is easy and cheap to make. It is durable and lightweight. Also the value of the paper is not related to the cost of materials to make it. Other products are stickers and T-shirts. Think of all the bumper stickers you have seen. Someone makes money selling these.

It can be difficult to find a niche in a market but it is important to identify one. Take the handmade paper example above. There is a huge market for printer paper and well established formats for paper sizes. You could sell handmade paper that conforms to the US Letter, A4 or A5 standard so it can be used in printers. This would be attractive to people who are prepared to pay a little extra for quality paper that has a distinctive texture and style. You could then target printing and copying companies, especially those that specialize in wedding invitations, for example. By identifying a niche you can avoid direct competition with larger players in the market.

Right now is the best time to start a business on eBay because eBay actually wants to attract individuals and businesses that sell multiple items at a fixed price. They want to move away from people who have just one item for sale by auction. Unfortunately eBay do not want drop shippers. I don't know why this is but eBay may change their policy in the future.

5 Ways to Make Money While You Sleep

Ok, so, like me, you are not good with handcrafts and have no artistic talents. How can you make money while you sleep on eBay? There are a couple of ways I know of to go about this. One way is to source products from eBay. You look for products that are undervalued, buy them and re-sell them for a profit. This method will suit someone who enjoys online shopping. It also takes talent to spot a bargain and know the intrinsic value of items. You will also need a little capital to get started but you can start right away. Consider buying items from other online sources and re-selling them on eBay. My advice here is to steer away from electronic goods like mobile phones and notebooks. Cheap electronic goods are often sold on eBay because they are not genuine. Steer clear of secondhand mobile phones and notebooks. You do not know what condition they are actually in or they could be stolen. Accessories for these items is likely to be a better option. A good place to look for bargains is in fashion and women's fashion accessories.

Another option is to go to local markets and look for products that fit the eBay model of lightweight and durable. This can have a very interesting outcome if you can get the right supplier/merchant. Consider this: you approach a merchant at a local market and enquire whether they can supply you with products in bulk at a reduced price. After you have established a strong business relationship with them, you ask if you can supply them with addresses to mail the items to. Or you ask them to supply products to a packaging and posting company. You then create a drop shipping business model. You no longer have to hold stock. All you are doing is filling orders and this can be done via email. Once the infrastructure is in place you can automate the email ordering step. This is now a money generator.

One of the easiest and cost effective ways to get started is to look around your own home for things you no longer use or perhaps have never used. Photograph these and list them on eBay.

A good friend of mine does quite well selling hunting accessories on eBay. He sources these items like rifle scopes, knives, tents and backpacks from China. He buys online and in bulk spending about $1000 at a time. He then lists the items on eBay. He tells me the sales are seasonal in that they tend to drop off as the hunting seasons start. Also he says that you have to be ready to lose the one thousand dollars as the Chinese suppliers can be unreliable. Take this as anecdotal advice as I have not personally done this. I include this simply as another avenue that you might like to try when looking for items to sell.

Why choose eBay? I suggest you start with eBay because they have a high volume of daily traffic. They are open 24/7 and the traffic is mainly people looking to buy.

5 Ways to Make Money While You Sleep

Qualified traffic. Think of eBay as the world's largest shopping mall and you are opening up a shop in that mall. That sounds flippant but you have to think in business terms. Get serious about making money while sleeping and persevere. Carefully consider your products. Choose lightweight and durable items. Do not rush out and buy 100 items of stock. Buy no more than 5 items to start with. Create high quality photos to post on eBay. When signing up for an account, choose a username related to the niche you want to fill. Once you have created your eBay account, look for other online auction sites and re-use the photos you posted on eBay. In other words, create several income streams. Then multiply the income streams by increasing the number of products you sell. You want to aim for about 100 products across 5 to 10 online auction sites.

At the time of writing this chapter in the first draft of this book eBay had a good reputation with sellers. This reputation has become tarnished and many sellers are moving to Amazon and Yahoo. I personally have nothing bad to say about eBay but I am aware that they have recently changed their policies regarding sellers. The information and advice contained in this chapter applies equally well to Amazon and Yahoo if you choose to sell on those sites. The important aspect of eBay is setting up the infrastructure to take money online. The webmail account and the PayPal account. I have sold books through Amazon before and they paid me by cheque in the mail. This is not a desirable payment method for an online money generator. I have no experience with Yahoo.

Because I have limited personal experience with Amazon and no experience with Yahoo I am not qualified to give advice on either website. However, as I have stated, you want to setup as many income streams as you can across several online auction sites. My advice is to keep an open mind. Try all three sites out and find as many more as you can. You can always drop a site in the future if you desire.

Always work towards the goal of supplying orders to a postage and packaging business or other third party. One word of caution. Remember the money has to flow from the internet to your bank account. Never post an item until you have received the payment. Beware the little old lady from Scotland who has a Gmail, Hotmail or Yahoo email address and a son who works for BP in Nigeria. There are scammers who frequent eBay. Never post items unless you receive payment first. If the person buying the item is requesting that you send the item to a postal address not associated with their account, use extreme caution. Wait until the money has cleared the PayPal payment process before sending the item.

5 Ways to Make Money While You Sleep

In Summary:

- EBay attracts large volumes of qualified traffic so you are likely to successfully sell just about any product through them.

- Look for products that are lightweight and durable to avoid having to refund or replace broken items.

- Try to identify a niche in a market to avoid competing against well-established sellers.

- Start small. Start with 1 product on 1 site. Increase the number of products, then increase the number of sites.

- Avoid holding large amounts of stock.

- EBay itself can be a good place to source items to sell. This is a good place to start.

- Local markets can be a good place to source goods to sell on eBay.

- Always work towards supplying orders to a postage and packaging business or other third party.

- Beware of scammers. Always make sure you receive the money before sending the goods.

Alister Rutledge

5 Ways to Make Money While You Sleep

Your Personal TV Station

YouTube is an excellent way to make money while sleeping. Videos on YouTube conform more to the money generator model I like, which is: Do something once and sell it a million times.

You make money on YouTube by advertising and merchandising just like any TV station. In order to create a successful money generator on YouTube you need to build a subscriber base. You attract subscribers by creating engaging content. You can also make the content interactive by requesting viewers to comment on the content of your videos. YouTube is a social network and people who frequent YouTube are called YouTubers.

To have a successful channel on YouTube you need to plan for success from the start. Choose the theme for your channel and the name for your channel at the same time. The name of your channel should reflect your theme. Since Google bought YouTube they want you to use your name as the name for your channel. This will suit some themes quite nicely but it may also stop your channel from standing out from the crowd. You can have just about any theme you want but I suggest you choose a topic you are interested in because you will spend hours talking about it. Politics, religion and current affairs do well on YouTube as these can be controversial and viewers like to comment about these topics. My advice is to never disable comments on your videos.

Once you have a theme, spend time and maybe money creating a logo and opening vignette for your videos. You can often hire graphic artists on Elance for very little cost to create a snappy opening vignette to use on every video. Consistency is very important to create a professional looking video. Make no mistake, you will be competing against big TV production houses on YouTube. I believe the individual has the advantage here because TV caters to the mainstream and is bound by regulations whereas the individual targets a niche and is not confined by the same regulations.

Always script your content. You are putting yourself out in the public domain on YouTube so do your research if you are going to be discussing politics, religion, science or something similar. Over time you can become an authority on your particular topic and this can lead to speaking engagements and the like on other forums. Make no mistake, you are more than likely to become a celebrity to some degree by putting your face on YouTube.

Consider creating a series of videos on a topic if your topic is broad. A series of short videos covering a broad topic is far more successful than one long rambling video. This also encourages viewers to come back to your

5 Ways to Make Money While You Sleep

channel. It also allows for viewers with slow internet connections or download limits to consume your content in bite size chunks.

If you have a trade, for instance you might be a mechanic, you should consider a series of videos on how to fix cars. By creating a series of short videos that are educational in nature you can get picked up by educational institutions. This can be very lucrative as your videos will become part of a teacher's toolkit and continue to be used every year. This gives you an excellent long-term income stream.

Edit your videos. You do not want long pauses and useless pans and zooms in your videos. Cut out anything that detracts from your content. Don't have long periods of no action that lead up to a couple of seconds of action. People will just switch to something more interesting. Remember the average attention span is 2 minutes and getting shorter every year. There are numerous free video editing software packages available on the web. A quick Google search will give you several options.

It has to be said that pretty, photogenic girls who show a bit of cleavage tend to be very successful on YouTube. This should not come as a surprise to anyone. It's the reason TV personalities aren't ugly old men. If you are shy or not photogenic you might want to consider employing someone to front your channel.

This leads to the topic of funding your money generator. The number one rule of making money while sleeping is that the money flows from the internet to your bank account. However, it is true that you need to spend money to make money. You do not need to spend your money to make money. There are several sites on the web that you can use to raise money to fund your endeavors. KickStarter and Pozible are two examples of sites that provide crowd funding. You basically pitch your idea to the crowd and request funding in return for some measure of your success. This is where your merchandizing can come in handy. You can offer coffee cups and t-shirts as incentives to donate to your project. This also gives you the opportunity to advertise your channel before it even starts. It is possible to raise several thousand and even tens of thousands of dollars through crowd funding.

Ok, so you're no good with a video camera, you have no interests worth talking about and you're an ugly old man that nobody wants to help. You can still create a money generator on YouTube. You can take content from YouTube itself and critique it. This depends on the publishing license so be careful about copyright infringement but most videos can be used for educational and analysis purposes. You can setup a channel that critiques other YouTube channels. A channel that features bloopers or "fails" will often attract many viewers. This is

5 Ways to Make Money While You Sleep

actually not a bad way to get started because getting seen on YouTube is not as easy as it used to be.

The stagnation of YouTube is often a topic discussed on YouTube. There are many well established YouTube channels that YouTube recommends to users. New channels that don't have a subscriber base are generally not recommended to viewers. This makes it difficult to start making money. The answer here is to not try to do things on your own. A successful strategy is to form a group of new content providers and cross promote your videos. Find a new channel that has a similar or opposing theme to yours and contact the owner. Make a loose agreement with them to cross promote your channels until you reach a certain number of subscribers. At the same time approach a well-established channel owner and ask them to give you a shout-out. Most old time YouTubers will give you a shout-out if your content is good enough. Shout-outs from YouTubers can boost your subscriber count overnight.

Subscribers are the key to making money on YouTube. Every time you post a new video to your channel YouTube emails your subscribers inviting them to view it. This is automatic and it drives people to your content which generates money for you. Also, when people reply to comments the original poster will be notified of the reply by YouTube. They visit your channel to view the comment and your video plays and displays the advertisement. That generates money for you. Never disable comments on your videos. After a while you can have hundreds of videos that people will email to each other. You can also put links on your videos that suggest more content for people to consume. So you cross promote older content. Once you have a subscriber base you can start merchandising in earnest.

Merchandising is something you should plan for from the start. When you are creating videos wear a T-shirt with your logo on it and maybe a pithy comment. Get a coffee cup that carries your logo and place it in shot while you address your audience. Get pens and caps made that carry your logo. Put a link at the bottom of your video that allows people to purchase your merchandise. And here's the clincher. Sell your merchandise on eBay and other auction sites. Selling merchandise online is going to cross promote your YouTube channel and get you more subscribers. You can see now that this is a big wheeled money generator that you are setting in motion.

T-shirts can be created on Teespring. It is free to create a range of t-shirts on teespring and you can sell them from teespring as well. The secret to success on teespring is traffic volume. Approximately 5% of people visiting your t-shirts will buy one. If you combine a YouTube channel, eBay listing, FaceBook fan page and email advertising campaign with a teespring offer you can drive qualified traffic to your t-shirts and expect to get about a 5%

5 Ways to Make Money While You Sleep

conversion rate. If you can drive 100,000 people to your t-shirt offer you can expect to make approximately $40,000 (that's at $8.00 profit per shirt). You can easily have one t-shirt campaign a month and make a very reasonable income. T-shirts are also a great way to advertise your YouTube channel. So make sure you include your logo or at least the name of your channel on your t-shirts. The more subscribers you get the easier it becomes to make money.

The holy grail of the YouTuber is the viral video. A video going viral is not something that just happens. Most often it is a carefully orchestrated advertising campaign. To get a video to go viral you need to have a short, quirky, funny and entertaining snippet that is going to appeal to a wide audience. You can actually find these on YouTube. A good example is the monkey on the pig video. The video had been on YouTube for years. Someone took it and created a song to go with it. It then went viral. Once you have the video on your channel, you advertise it.

Use social media like Facebook, Twitter and Tumblr to get it seen by your friends and their friends. At the same time get it emailed around the world. You do this by going to a site like Fiverr and searching on the word "traffic". You will find many people who will send a link in an email to thousands of people for just five dollars. My advice is to avoid offers that say they will send unlimited emails. Often this means that they will send to

40 or 50 email addresses each day for a month. Choose people who will send to a quoted number of email addresses. Choose several of these people. You are looking for people who will send a minimum of 1000 emails and you want at least 6 of them. The point here is that the link to the video is now in thousands of emails. This makes it easy for people to forward the email to their friends and on and on it goes. The social media links re-enforce the emailed links. Pretty soon you have 1 million people viewing your video. This gets picked up by mainstream media and things really snowball. The ultimate goal is to get a report about your video mentioned on the nightly news.

The nightly news can be a good source for content. You can record just about any commercial or cable TV program and, as long as you are using it as a basis for analysis or criticism, re-use it. This comes under the fair use clause in copyright law. As long as you are adding content to the original, you should be safe from litigation.

One of the most important things to do to create a successful channel is to regularly upload new content. You should schedule this and tell your subscribers that you will release new videos every week or month as the case may be. Forming a professional, business like, yet friendly and entertaining relationship with your subscribers is probably the most important ingredient to a successful YouTube channel.

5 Ways to Make Money While You Sleep

Whatever you do on YouTube, you will attract people who are going to react negatively to your content. They are going to leave nasty comments and probably create video responses to your channel. Grow a thicker hide. These people are trolls but they will actually help to promote your content by attracting attention to you. Remember this is a business. It's not personal. You are setting the channel up to make money first above all.

In Summary

- Subscribers are your customers.

- Attract subscribers through engaging content and always allowing comments on your channel.

- Choose the theme and name for your channel at the same time.

- Spend time and maybe money creating an opening vignette or catchy logo that you display on every video.

- Invest in and learn how to use editing software.

- Always script your videos.

- Merchandize your channel from the start.

- Use other YouTubers to cross promote your channel.

- Try to get shout-outs from more established YouTubers.

- Use FaceBook, Twitter and other blog sites to promote your channel.

- Consider crowd funding to generate capital if required.

- Regularly upload new content to your channel.

The Best Seller

Everybody has a book in them and it has never been easier to publish than right now. The site lulu.com allows you to publish traditional books and e-books. The great thing about lulu is that it distributes to Amazon and Barnes & Noble, two well-known book stores.

Books are excellent money generators because you put the effort in once and sell it a million times. Books also sell for a long time so you get income for several years. Putting the effort in takes time but you can do it in your spare time.

There are two formats to consider at the moment. There is the traditional hardcover or paperback book and the electronic or e-book that people download onto their e-book reader like Kindle. These are two distinct formats that have different formatting requirements. If you choose to publish a traditional book, I suggest you download a template from lulu. These are word document templates and come in a variety of sizes. If you choose to publish an e-book I suggest you download the Calibre e-book management studio. If you don't have Microsoft Office you can use the free alternative from Sun Microsystems called Open Office. This is open source software that can open Microsoft Word documents.

An e-book style is different to a paperback style and the two are really not interchangeable. E-books tend to be shorter in length so if you have a lot to say you should consider a paperback or hardcover. Traditionally you published in hardcover first and then released a paperback version. This is not the case today. Most books come out in paperback first. They are easier to post.

So, what to write about? I am going to assume that you, like myself, are not another J. K. Rawlings and don't have a Harry Potter inside you waiting to come out. If you consider the previous chapter and you thought of a theme for your YouTube channel, you have a theme for a book. Also you can cross promote your book on your YouTube channel. You could consider writing about your experiences in creating your YouTube channel. Really the possibilities are endless.

Let's look more closely at e-books because they are a lot shorter and therefore quicker to write and publish. Because there are so many possibilities for e-books I'm going to take stamp collecting as an example. Let's say that your hobby is stamp collecting and you belong to a stamp collecting group. You decide to write an e-book called "The Definitive Guide to Stamp Collecting". A tome that is all things stamp collecting. This is a good start but it actually contains several other books. You could then write another e-book called "Seven Common Mistakes in Collecting Stamps." What about "Stamp

5 Ways to Make Money While You Sleep

Collecting for Beginners" and "Expert Stamp Collecting."? What about "The Five Best Stamps to Collect."? You now have 5 e-books and you can go on. "The Five Worst Stamps to Avoid Collecting.".

You can see where I'm going with this. Every book is an income stream. Now consider translating all those books into Simplified Chinese, Hindi, Spanish, French and German. You now have 36 income streams. Translation is easy and free using Google Translate. At the time of writing it is my understanding that the epub format is only available in English but pdf supports multiple languages.

Let's say that you know nothing and therefore it is impossible for you to publish an e-book. Well you'd be wrong. You may not be an expert but there are plenty of experts ready and willing to educate you on their topic of expertise. All you have to do is find them and interview them. Universities are good places to find experts. Contact them and request an interview. Tell them you are writing a book on their subject. Be up front about it and give them an acknowledgment in the book. Ask if you can record the interview. Then look at breaking the interview material down into several e-books. A word of advice. Get yourself prepared for the interview. Do your homework and put together 100 pertinent questions. Don't go in there expecting to be able to wing it. An expert's time is valuable and they are not going to waste it on trivial questions.

Let's say you know nothing but you've interviewed your expert and have plenty of material. You just need to write it down but you don't have time or you can't write to save yourself. You can still publish your e-books. You go to Elance and hire a freelance writer. This is going to cost you about 800 dollars and you will need to supply a rough draft or at least some copy for them to work with. It will also take about a week to complete. Do not just supply them with the transcript of the interview. Once you have contacted a freelance writer they can tell you what they require from you.

The market for e-books is already large and growing rapidly. This means there is competition for readership. You want to generate money as fast as you can. Start to publicize your e-books before you publish them. Facebook and Twitter are obvious places to start. Generate interest by telling your friends and followers that you are writing several books and give them sneak previews. Start a Tumblr blog if you don't already have one. Crowd funding is not just a way to get capital, it is also a way to publicize your e-books. You can offer free copies of the books in return for funding.

Make your e-books self-promoting. E-books are published under several licensing policies. One of these

5 Ways to Make Money While You Sleep

policies is a reseller license. There are people who buy only resalable e-books. Publish one of the e-books under a reseller license. Put references to the other e-books in this book. Something like a list of books by this author. The reseller will then help you to promote your books. If you make your resalable e-book a free download, you will get more downloads and more publicity for your other e-books.

Another way to generate interest in your books is to write e-zine articles about your subject matter and reference your e-books by title in the references section at the end of the article. Do not include URLs to your books in the body of the e-zine article. Most e-zine sites will not publish an article full of URLs. Just Google search e-zines to find the popular sites.

You can use Elance and Fiverr to find people who specialize in writing e-zine articles. Do not be shy about using other people to produce or market your books. This is a very well established method for producing copy. Think of it this way: This is a business. You are the CEO and you are employing contractors to get your business off the ground.

Another avenue to use to market your books is book revues. Again go to Fiverr to find people who will review your books and also publish the review to blog sites and sites that specialize in book reviews. These blogs and book review sites are frequented by book-worms. This is your market. You need to get your book in front of as many users as you can.

Use Fiverr to email links to your books and to your e-zine articles. A great way to publicize your e-books is on local talk back radio. Most talk back stations can give you a phone interview, particularly if your subject matter is topical or controversial.

What to write about? This is a difficult question to answer. It really comes down to whether you are writing a book to make money or to get your personal point of view across to the public at large. Books that do well and are not controversial are things like recipe books, especially if you combine them with a health or weight loss slant. "How to" books do well. Things like "How to Tile Your Bathroom". These also lead to titles like "5 Things to Avoid When Tiling Your Bathroom". Controversial topics like politics and religion can back fire on you. You should consider appealing to the tastes of the largest section of a niche. In the case of religion, you are probably going to sell more copies if you tell people what they want to hear rather than disparage closely held beliefs. Richard Dawkins and Christopher Hitchens are probably two notable exceptions to that statement.

My advice is to start small. Get a book published so you learn the requirements of the lulu site. Then plan your

5 Ways to Make Money While You Sleep

strategic cornering of a market. Start the marketing campaign before you release your titles. Use social media, e-zines, blogs and crowd funding to generate interest and to sustain the interest after publication. Publish at least one reseller title. Also, make your reseller title a free download.

Once you are published, use Fiverr to help promote your books. You may want to consider creating a website to help promote your books. A good place to start is WordPress. It is free to setup a WordPress site. Wix.com is a free website builder and site hosting service. More advanced website features are not free with Wix.

My general advice is to avoid building a website as much as possible and you certainly do not need a website to publish books. However, even the most popular books do not stay at the top of the bestseller lists forever. With books you want to get as many residual sales as possible. A website can help you with this. A website that lists and promotes your books will help maintain your income streams for some time into the future. It will also be indexed by the search engines which will make your books easier to find on the web.

Although there are several very good options to building and hosting websites, this should be left to the second phase of your marketing campaign. Websites take a lot of work to setup. You should focus your efforts on producing as many books as you can. Also, you need to have the books published in order to list them on a website. So my advice is to plan to eventually have your books listed on your own website but leave the details and work involved until you are ready to implement the second phase of your marketing campaign.

If you have never built a website, my advice is to leave it to the experts. Again you are the CEO. Contract someone who specializes in websites to build one for you. Avoid people who want to build and host the site for you as you will end up paying hosting fees. You want to find a person who will supply you with the required files and upload them to a free hosting site. Elance is the place to go to find website developers. I do not know the costs involved here as I build and host my own websites.

In Summary

- Printed books and e-books have different formatting requirements

- Use templates from lulu to write traditional books.

- Look for templates that will give you the largest global reach.

5 Ways to Make Money While You Sleep

- Use Calibre e-book Management Studio to produce e-books.

- With e-books, try to create as many titles around a single theme as possible.

- Produce e-books related to a YouTube channel or eBay business to cross promote your income streams.

- Always have one re-seller licensed e-book that lists other e-books within a group of e-book titles.

- Use blogs and social media sites to generate interest in your books before, during and after you publish.

Alister Rutledge

The Killer App

Mobile phone and tablet apps are revenue generators that I am currently pursuing. The model here is similar to a cross between YouTube advertising and publishing e-books. There are three main ways to generate money while you sleep. The first is to sell the app directly in the same way you sell a book. Another way is to advertise within the app. The third way to generate income is in-app purchasing. Combining advertising and selling the app is frowned upon by the app community. Google recommends combining advertising and in app purchasing as the best way to generate income.

Selling an app as a one off purchase is actually not the best way to go about generating money. The purchasing of the app is actually a hurdle to download. People are reluctant to spend even a small, nominal amount of money on an app, where as they will spend the same or more purchasing a book. I find this difficult to understand as downloading apps opens your device up to installing malware. Purchasing an app is, in my opinion, far more secure as there is a well reported and monitored link back to the developer. However, until people wise up to just how invasive malware on a phone is, I think the free download model is more lucrative.

In-app purchasing works well with certain models. For example a gambling app or a game that requires you to

5 Ways to Make Money While You Sleep

purchase items to enhance your gaming experience. Many dating apps are free to download but require you to purchase the ability to communicate. In-app purchasing works well if you provide a service that has strong inducements to buy. The free download removes the hurdle to install. Many people do not like the shock of having to then purchase something to make the app work as advertised. This can generate negative comments which then slow the install rate. At the time of writing I have not tried in-app purchasing.

My experience to date has been with Android app development. If you choose to develop for iPhone this information should still be relevant. Firstly, you do not need to be a math genius to develop software. You just need to be able to think logically. All the 3rd generation programming languages have very simple logical constructs that determine what action is to be performed. If you can think in terms of "if condition X is true then perform action A" you have mastered the basics of programming apps for phones or tablets. You can then extend that to "if condition X is true then perform action A, else perform action B". That leads on to "while condition X is true perform action A" or "perform action A until condition X is true". I suggest that just about anybody can learn to program in about 6 months. There are numerous courses online that are very good but you can easily purchase a book like "Programming for

Dummies" to give you a good start in developing your first app.

Alternatively you can just download the required software and dive straight in. To start programming, download an IDE (Integrated Development Environment). For Android apps you need the Eclipse Android IDE. It is free to download. It also comes with a large number of virtual devices that you use to test apps on so you don't need to own an android device to write Android software. Android apps use a combination of XML and Java. XML stands for Extensible Markup Language and is used to define the user interface for an app. Java is a very good 3rd generation software language that uses an Object Orientated Design (OOD). Here's the trick. Almost every problem you come across in app development has been encountered by someone else. Not only that, developers like to tell each other about how to solve these problems. There are countless developer forums that will give you code examples about how to solve almost any issue you face. Be aware that these code examples are frequently incomplete and usually do not include error handlers. Using it as is will likely result unstable apps.

Don't let this put you off. Cut and paste the code examples into your IDE. Resolve the errors and add the error handlers. Debugging in Eclipse is a breeze. It compiles on the fly so it detects the errors for you and then gives you a list of options to resolve the issues.

5 Ways to Make Money While You Sleep

When you select the correct solution it writes the code for you.

Google has extensive documentation online about everything Android that also includes tutorials. There are also lots of Android tutorials online that take you step by step through the code required to do just about anything you can imagine.

The ads are very easy to add to your apps. You download the Google Play Services SDK (Software Development Kit) using the Eclipse Android SDK Manager and import the relevant classes into the IDE. Log on to Admob.com using your Google account and register your app. This will give you an app ID that you then plug into your advertising classes. When the app runs it is served ads from admob.com. The ads are HTML5 postage stamp size inserts that you can place on the screen. You are paid per view and per click. Full documentation can be found in the Google Android tutorials.

Still not convinced or unwilling to give software development a try. You can hire very highly qualified app developers on eLance.com. These tend to Indian programmers who are mostly university graduates. They are talented and very keen to work for foreign currency. Hiring programmers is going to require you to carefully consider ROI. Before you approach a programmer consider every requirement your app will need. Put together a design document and make sure you thoroughly cover all aspects of your app. One of the reasons I got out of the web development game was people who hired me knew less about web design than me but insisted on including items or pages that were either not required or poorly thought out. A developer is going to treat changes to the initial design as extras and will simply charge you extra for them. They are not going to worry too much about the usability of the app, only that they have met all the requirements of the design document.

What apps to create? There are a couple of ways to go about finding apps to create. Firstly look for what people or businesses need. It can be difficult for people without software development experience to see how a requirement can be met with an app. You need to be aware of the limitations of current technology. Reading technology news items and going to technology expos is a good way to keep abreast of the latest developments. Talking to other developers and joining a developers group or forum is also a fun way to keep up with trends in the app community.

Another option is to look at what is available on the app store and try to improve the apps already available. Pay particular attention to the reviews for apps as this will help with ideas about improving an existing app. In other words, you try to build a better mouse trap.

5 Ways to Make Money While You Sleep

You may want to use a Java de-compiler to reconstruct the class files from the binary executable. I haven't tried this with java but there are stand alone and plugin de-compilers available on the web. Be careful about legal restrictions when using other people's code. Decompiling applications is a legitimate way to learn about coding techniques.

When you are ready to publish your app, you go to the Google Play store and scroll to the bottom of the page. Right at the bottom there is a "developers" link. You need to have a Google account to sign in. After you logon on you will be taken to a splash page that informs you of the latest developments in the Android operating system. There is a menu at the top right of this page. Click the link taking you to the developer's console. Follow the steps to publish your app. You will need several screen caps of your app and a few promotional images.

The developer's console also allows you to enter your bank account details so you can be paid. Payments are made on or about the 15th of the month. There are a host of other tools available for analyzing your app's performance.

What sort of money can be made with apps? That depends on your payment model. A free app with 100,000 downloads will generate approximately USD $1250 per day. That's a reasonable income. Not every app is going to get 100,000 downloads so you need to employ a strategy to reach that number. The strategy I am using is very similar to the e-book strategy. I create an app and then translate it into several languages. This enables me to target different markets. I translate into Hindi and Mandarin to reach the huge Indian and Chinese markets. I also translate into Korean and Thai as these two Asian markets have a high proportion of mobile devices in use to their population sizes.

One of the benefits I have found with apps is that you don't really need to advertise them. People actively seek them out and downloads start a few days after the apps have been published. Another benefit is they don't age the same way books do. Apps I wrote last year are still being downloaded so I am getting a good residual income from them.

In Summary

- Income is derived from direct sales, advertising and in-app purchasing

- Learn to develop software. It's free and will enable you to keep your costs to a minimum.

- If required, you can hire developers easily online.

5 Ways to Make Money While You Sleep

- Get ideas for apps from friends, family and businesses. Google Play can be a source for ideas.

- Look at translating apps to different languages to increase your income streams.

- Apps have a long shelf life.

Alister Rutledge

Online Trading

This is my favorite way to make money while I sleep! It is also the riskiest. I use the etoro.com trading site. This is forex trading so it will not be to everyone's taste. Etoro has a very good user interface but is clunky over slow connections due to the reliance on Flash. You get a practice account of $10,000 when you sign up. It is free to sign up. There are extensive tutorials available on the site so you can learn the basics very quickly. Once you are ready, you switch to your real account. You need to fund this account but you can start with as little as $50 dollars. This is a great way to start and slowly build your equity. After a few weeks you can withdraw the $50 and your trading becomes self-funding. It is great to sit at your PC and watch the money come rolling in! I still get a kick out of it.

A spin off that I think is really worthwhile is that you find yourself becoming very interested in news about the indexes and share market fluctuations. The price of gold and oil suddenly becomes interesting. Changes in global politics become talking points with friends and colleagues. You take a wider interest in the world around you.

Etoro.com also has a social network called OpenBook. Here you can talk online with other traders and get tips on investments. You can also copy trade. This means that

5 Ways to Make Money While You Sleep

you can link your etoro account with an experienced trader and automatically make or lose money as the case may be. The site repeatedly tells you "past performance is no guarantee of future success" so you copy trade at your own risk. However, if you choose to copy the right trader things can get very exciting.

I cannot give you financial advice as I am not qualified to do so but, I will tell you the current strategy I use to make money by trading with etoro. I select several professional or experienced traders to copy. I do this by looking at their stats on their OpenBook profiles. I look for traders that make a decent and consistent monthly return and manually trade the majority of the time. I don't pay much attention to what they write about themselves on their profile. The stats don't lie. I copy their trades with $50 to start with. This is the minimum copy amount. When you copy a trader you are able to see what positions they take and what instruments they are using. I look at the take profit point they set to give me an indication of whether they are going long or short on the position. Here's where it gets interesting. Experienced traders make mistakes. They will take a buy position on an instrument when they should have taken a sell position. So I take the sell position and put $100 on it. I set my take profit point at 10% and go short. Invariably I will make $10 within the hour. Five of these short positions gives me $50. I usually put the small amount down because I assume the professional knows more about the trade than I do. I don't know why they took the original position but I can see the instrument trending the opposite way. So I take an opportunistic approach and grab a quick 10% return on investment. I do this while I am writing apps or surfing the web. I don't just sit and trade. I'm making about $50 an hour just sitting at my PC doing whatever I want! Sometimes I will know more about why an instrument has gone the wrong way for them so I can safely put a larger amount on the opposite position. I will usually look for a 20-30% return but still go short.

Often the experienced trader will take the correct position and you can see this. The instrument will go the right way and their take profit point will give them greater than 100% return on investment. I wait until there is at least a 10% change in the right direction and then put $1000 dollars on the same position and set the take profit at 50% return. This is a longer position but usually I will take profit within 3 to 4 hours. Sometimes a position will run for a day or two. Occasionally the trend will reverse before it reaches the take profit and this is why it is important to monitor your trades. If the position reverses significantly, I close it. It's better to take a couple of hundred dollars on a short than lock up one thousand dollars for several days. I look for another position to take with the one thousand dollars. When I am ready for bed I will put a couple of "safe" trades on for amounts that I

5 Ways to Make Money While You Sleep

can afford to lose. So if I've made a couple of thousand dollars during the day, I'll put five hundred dollars across several trades and set the take profit at 20-25%. When I wake up I'll log on and look at how much I've made. Usually the trades have closed but occasionally one or two are still running. I choose whether or not to close them.

If you build your equity up, or are prepared to invest several thousand dollars to start with, you can easily make $200 USD per day, 5 days a week. Not a bad income or way to make some spending money. Etoro also has an app so you can trade anywhere, anytime from your phone. The app lacks some details that are available on the website so my strategy is to place my trades using the website and then monitor them on my phone if I am away from my PC.

That's the strategy I use. You can adopt it and adapt it to your circumstances as required. I share my current strategy with you for informational purposes only and you should not take it as financial advice. You trade at your own risk.

Etoro has recently introduced a popular trader angle to their site. If you become a popular trader, Etoro will pay you 10,000 dollars per month. The details of how to become a popular trader are available on the website.

In Summary

- This is the only way I know of to reliably make instant money.

- This is also the riskiest way to make money online that I have tried.

- If you are new to trading, make use of the tutorials and practice account.

Conclusion

Outlined above are five ways to make money while sleeping that I personally have found to be successful. None of them require experience on the web and none require large investments of capital to get up and running. With the exception of etoro they all require an investment in time. This is important to understand. Hopefully this book will drive you to find other ways to create money generators. One rule of thumb is beware of the sure fire path to success that requires little or no effort on your behalf. There are plenty of people offering an easy path to success. I don't believe there is one.

The information I have provided in this book has been kept fairly generalized because I cannot provide the reader with specific information due to the fact I don't know your specific circumstances. I have deliberately avoided giving details about costs involved with eBay because eBay change their pricing policies from time to time. If I were to write them down, there is a good chance that the information would be out of date or inaccurate by the time you read this book.

I think it is fair to say that the biggest hurdle to success we all face is ourselves. Often fear of the risks involved can stop us from starting. All of the money generators outlined above take little or no money to get started. The risks are kept to a minimum. Remember the golden rule.

The money flows from the web to your bank account. Not the other way around. If you find that people are requiring money up front to perform a service or you have a limited time to take up an offer, look at where the money is flowing and remember the golden rule.

One of the keys to success on the web is traffic. All of the sites listed above, eBay, Amazon, Google Play and YouTube are well known and have huge volumes of daily traffic. By using them you are assured that your endeavors will be seen by lots of people. Beware of schemes from unknown sites that promise rich rewards. Unless there is a lot of traffic visiting that site it would be hard to justify the claim.

If I can give you any advice it would be to start small but plan for success. Always carefully consider ROI. Choose a single money generator and pursue that until you generate a return on investment. Then diversify into other money generators. Along the way you will encounter setbacks and difficulties. Learn from these setbacks. Find out why you have experienced difficulties and learn to avoid them in the future. Remember; if you give up you definitely fail. If you keep trying you just haven't succeeded yet. The rewards are worth making the effort for.

What are the rewards? The rewards are being able to live the life you have the way you want to live it. Not to be

5 Ways to Make Money While You Sleep

tied down to a job that offers false security while demanding one third of your life. To be able to wake up and truly ask yourself "What do I want to do today?"

Appendix 1

Use the following pages for research and planning.

For eBay you want to research your market looking for your niche. Decide whether you are going to sell new products or re-sell products you find on eBay or other auction sites. Can you source products from a local market?

For YouTube you want to think about what your channel is going to be about. Are you going to provide educational content, new content on specific or generalized information or are you going to source content from YouTube and critique it. What merchandizing can you do? Can you incorporate that merchandizing on your eBay listing or will you have a separate eBay listing for merchandizing? Will you be able to get crowd funding for your channel?

What e-book topics can you think of? Can these topics be broken down into several related topics? Will you write the books or do you need to have them written for you? If someone else will write them, how much will that cost? Can you get crowd funding for this?

What ideas for apps can you come up with? Will you write the apps yourself? If not, how much will it cost to have them written for you? How will this affect your return on investment?

5 Ways to Make Money While You Sleep

Alister Rutledge

5 Ways to Make Money While You Sleep

Alister Rutledge

5 Ways to Make Money While You Sleep

Planning for Success

eBay		
Products	Cost	Sell price including P&H

Username	
Password	

Alister Rutledge

Supplier Contact Information		
Name	Phone	Email

5 Ways to Make Money While You Sleep

YouTube	
Channel Name	
User Name	
Password	

Cross Promotional Contacts	
Channel Name	Email Address

Alister Rutledge

Notes

5 Ways to Make Money While You Sleep

eBooks	
Title	Synopsis

Alister Rutledge

Lulu details	
Username	
Password	

Fiverr Contacts	
Name	Contact Info

5 Ways to Make Money While You Sleep

	Apps
Name	Purpose

Alister Rutledge

Google Play Account	
Username	
Password	

Notes

Glossary

ClickBank – www.clickbank.com – A global network of over 100,000 affiliate marketers.

Drop Ship Source Directory - http://www.worldwidebrands.com/ - A resource for drop shippers and wholesalers.

eBay - http://www.ebay.com – Online auction site.

YouTube - http://www.youtube.com/ - Online video hosting site with a social network.

Teespring - http://teespring.com/ - Online T-Shirts for merchandising and selling.

Elance - https://www.elance.com – An online resource for freelance writers, programmers and marketers.

KickStarter - https://www.kickstarter.com – A site for crowd funding.

Pozible - http://www.pozible.com – A site for crowd funding.

Fiverr - http://www.fiverr.com – A site for freelancers who can help promote your endeavors.

Tumblr - https://www.tumblr.com – Blogging with a social network.

Calibre - http://calibre-ebook.com – e-book management software.

Open Office - https://www.openoffice.org – Free office software suite.

Lulu - http://www.lulu.com – Publishing and distribution site.

WordPress - http://wordpress.com – Blogging and website builder.

Wix.com - http://www.wix.com - Free website building and hosting service.

5 Ways to Make Money While You Sleep

Eclipse - https://www.eclipse.org/downloads/ - Free integrated development environment

Admob - http://www.admob.com/login/ - A source for in-app advertising.

Kilobolt - http://www.kilobolt.com/day-1-foundations - A very good tutorial site for developing games and learning programming.

Etoro - http://www.etoro.com.au/webtrader - Online trading site.

OpenBook - https://openbook.etoro.com – Social network for etoro.com.

www.ingramcontent.com/pod-product-compliance
Lightning Source LLC
Chambersburg PA
CBHW072232170526
45158CB00002BA/856